RETURN AND CONTINUE WITH HONOR

"*Return and Continue with Honor* contains amazingly helpful suggestions for every returning missionary. I wish a resource like this had been available when I returned from my mission."

—**AMANDA BURTON**, Taiwan Taichung Mission

"This booklet is almost like my missing companion. It understands what a returned missionary is going through. It makes connections that those around you often don't recognize. It gives a sense of assurance because what I was going through was written on the pages."

—**CADEN CARPENTER**, Washington
Kennewick Mission

"I really love all the activities included in this booklet because we as missionaries need things to do when fresh home. Having something wholesome and worthwhile to do is stabilizing for an RM."

—**KATIE LOFTUS**, Uruguay Montevideo Mission

"I am still trying to apply a lot of these principles in my life. This booklet has given me helpful direction that I needed for a better transition as a returned missionary."

—**COREY BREINHOLT**, Provo Utah Mission

"I am so thankful for this book. Each section helped me expand on what my mission president instructed me to do when I returned home. It gave me the confidence I needed to go out into the world and continue to become the woman I grew to be on the mission."

—**BRITTNEY BREINHOLT**, Atlanta Georgia North Mission

"From Primary to the MTC, Church members are given plentiful assistance and guidance regarding mission preparation, but there is not much in the way of help for returning missionaries until now. The information in *Return and Continue with Honor* is presented in a logical and sequential format that is easy to comprehend and to put into practice."

—**DAIN KNUDSON**, San Antonio Texas Mission

"I wish that I'd had this when I had come home. I can attest that I truly felt the way this booklet described. This will help any family or returned missionary to adjust to this new life."

—**JT HOPPINS**, Las Vegas Nevada Mission

RETURN AND CONTINUE WITH HONOR

A GUIDE FOR RETURNING MISSIONARIES

RETURN AND CONTINUE
WITH
HONOR

A GUIDE FOR RETURNING MISSIONARIES

BROCK BOOHER

CFI
An Imprint of Cedar Fort, Inc.
Springville, Utah

ISBN 13: 978-1-4621-1683-6

Published by CFI, an imprint of Cedar Fort, Inc.
2373 W. 700 S., Springville, UT 84663
Distributed by Cedar Fort, Inc., www.cedarfort.com

LIBRARY OF CONGRESS CATALOGING-IN-PUBLICATION DATA

Booher, Brock, 1963- author.
Return and continue with honor / Brock Booher.
    pages cm
ISBN 978-1-4621-1683-6
1. Mormon missionaries--Conduct of life. 2. Mormons--Conduct of life. 3. Adjustment (Psychology)--Religious aspects--Church of Jesus Christ of Latter-day Saints. I. Title.

BX8661.B66 2015
266'.9332--dc23

                              2014046062

Cover design by Shawnda T. Craig
Cover design © 2015 Lyle Mortimer
Edited and typeset by Kevin Haws

Printed in the United States of America

10 9 8 7 6 5 4 3 2 1

Printed on acid-free paper

DEDICATION

To those who have served as full-time missionaries and struggled to find their place in the culture of the Church as returned missionaries.

CONTENTS

ACKNOWLEDGMENTS

SOME TIME AGO, I was at my friend Shane Bennett's house, welcoming home his son after a mission in Peru. The event struck an emotional chord with me and I began to lament the plight of returned missionaries and the struggles they face. I explained how alone I felt when I came home over thirty years ago, and I still felt the emotional sting of the experience. My friend Brent Martindale looked at me, shrugged, and said, "You're a writer. Write a book."

The idea hit me with incredible energy, and for several days afterward I couldn't stop thinking about it. I felt prompted to move on it, but self-doubt crept in. After all, who was I to write advice for returned missionaries? I'm not an expert. I have no credentials. The project scared me to death and I felt inadequate to even begin working on it. I went the opposite direction and focused on writing fiction.

Acknowledgments

My wife, Britt, believed in me though, and every time I started a new writing project she encouraged and prodded me to write this. Eventually, I received a Church calling working directly with returned missionaries and could no longer ignore the promptings or run away from the project.

I wrote this book for the young men and women returning from missionary service in our stake. My good stake president, Ron Derrick, and I talked at length about the content. His wise counsel guided me. Karl Mann encouraged me. Todd Nuttall, a fellow missionary from my mission in Uruguay, prodded me to finish. Carl Burgess and I laughed at some of the awkward moments we both had faced as newly returned missionaries. My friend Wade Whiting discussed with me the problems that returned missionaries in his stake faced and helped me flesh out the manuscript. My friend Leroy Breinholt energetically supported my efforts so that he would have a tool to use with all the returned missionaries in the singles stake. My writing group—Randy Lindsay, Ryan Hancock, Stephen Stirling, Adrienne Quintana, Laura Walker, Janette Rallison, and especially Shersta Chabot (she forced me to look deeper)—all made my writing better. My friend and neighbor Alan Wilson talked with me until the early morning about life and the challenges of adult children. LuAnn Roundy provided the insight that only a professional counselor can provide. And of course, I owe a great debt to all the returned missionaries that took the time to give me feedback.

To say that I wrote this book would be a lie. I put it together, but I pulled from the wisdom of friends, family, and Church leaders. I also felt the guidance of the Spirit through the process.

When Emily Chambers emailed me and let me know that Cedar Fort wanted to publish my book, I was ecstatic and scared to death. I wanted to run away again. Instead, I asked for prayers from friends and family members. With heaven's help, I finished this in time to meet my deadline.

It has been thirty years, but I can still remember that empty feeling I felt when I walked off the airplane after my mission. I hope that this book will make it easier for all the wonderful young men and women coming home to deal with the transition from full-time missionary to faithful returned missionary.

INTRODUCTION

I WATCHED THE young missionary's face as he came down the aisle of the airplane looking for his seat. The worn suit and slightly faded black name tag were dead giveaways. He was going home. He had a content look in his eyes, but an anxious one on his face. He seemed confident and yet somewhat unsettled. He shuffled past me, courteous with everyone. No doubt he wasn't the same young man that had said goodbye to family and friends two years ago. He had finished his missionary service and was going home, but home to what?

If he were like many returning missionaries and had grown up in the Church, he had been preparing to be a missionary for much of his life. Since he was a young boy in Primary, he had been constantly encouraged to serve a full-time mission. During his years in the Young

Men's program, he'd been interviewed, examined, and inculcated with the responsibility of serving the Lord as a full-time missionary. His mission had been the focal point of his future for most of his life, and now it was over, just like that.

As a church, we do an incredible job of preparing young men and women to serve missions. We enroll them in seminary. We take them on spiritual retreats that we call campouts. We encourage missionary service in Sunday School lessons, priesthood lessons, and family home evenings. We reiterate it in bishopric interviews and patriarchal blessings. We send them to mission prep classes and spend hours preparing our young men and women for the rigors of missionary life.

We don't miss any opportunity to encourage our young men to serve missions, and even though the same pressure isn't applied to our young women, we tell them of the blessings of full-time missionary service and encourage them to serve as well. But we don't stop there. We also ask our young women to encourage young men to serve as missionaries and not date them seriously until afterward.

In Church social circles, we talk about missionaries who are leaving, missionaries who are currently serving, and missionaries who are coming home. We hold open houses when they leave to serve, have missionary mom luncheons while they're gone, and big dinner celebrations when they return. The full-time missionary experience is a rite of passage and an integral part of Church doctrine, policy, and culture.

Even after all the insistence and training done with the family, ward, and stake, once young men or women show up at the Missionary Training Center, the real preparation begins. They spend all their waking hours in classrooms, devotionals, or personal study preparing to go forth and serve. They are taught gospel principles and how to explain them to others. They figure out how to deal with difficult objections and strange questions. They learn the language and culture of their assigned area. They are immersed in the Spirit and hopefully listen to the promptings and whispers that testify of truth. They receive all the necessary resources for them to succeed including books, teachers, computer-based learning programs, role-playing partners, mentors, and ecclesiastical guidance. Nothing is spared in the training of new missionaries.

When new missionaries arrive in the field, all the training and support continue. Along with having a companion, they are assigned a training leader, a district leader, zone leaders, assistants to the president, and the mission president and his wife. Every week, they attend a district meeting or a zone conference. They are monitored and held accountable for their statistical numbers that represent the work they have done. They sit down with their companions to discuss progress, struggles they are having, and air out any conflicts. They are regularly interviewed by the mission president and given guidance, should they need it.

The structure of the mission surrounds and supports the missionaries as they struggle to stand on their own two feet. It nurtures and grooms them as they progress and prepare for more responsibility and leadership. The missionary is never left alone to struggles and hardships that inevitably come as a missionary.

Then suddenly they are walking off the airplane in that well-worn suit or dress and faded black name tag into the arms of family and other loved ones as returned missionaries. The stake president meets with and releases them. They make a report to the high council. They speak in sacrament meeting. Everyone pats them on the back and asks them, "How was your mission?" (Like the experience could be described like yesterday's lunch.) Friends and family members stop by to welcome them home and congratulate them. Parents bask in the renewal of the relationship. For a few weeks, everyone is caught up in the novelty of the newly returned missionary.

A few weeks later, they are sitting alone on their parents' couch or in their bedroom. No companion is there. Nobody is asking them for reports. There is no looming interview or appointment to race to. Returned missionaries face one of the most difficult challenges of the mission: coming home. And they often face it alone.

The once zealous young men and women that have sacrificed years of their time and postponed schooling, careers, and personal goals may now find themselves drifting aimlessly, looking for some kind of cause. After suffering hot days, cold nights, and rude people in order to share their testimonies, they now feel unneeded, or even unwanted. The returned missionaries who just a few months ago would have taken a bullet for the Church feel like nothing they do will ever measure up to what they have already accomplished.

These returned missionaries went forth with faith and won the battle, and now—like war heroes—they return from the front lines, trailing honor, still wielding the sword of truth. They are soldiers without a cause, feeling like veritable Don Quixotes, all searching for windmills to charge.

Now is when they are most vulnerable. This is when we are most likely to see them slip into inactivity. Our heroic young men and women conquered long days of rejection or even persecution, but they could succumb to the insidious evil of having nothing worthwhile to focus on. They might fall prey to a lack of meaningful purpose. They will flounder looking for a cause as worthy as spreading the gospel while they try to navigate the maze of life after their mission.

Fast forward a few years and you might find a young father struggling to make ends meet, no longer active in the Church because he "just can't find the time," or suffers from some other crisis of faith. You might find a young woman that is no longer worthy of temple blessings because she has slipped up. You might even find a rebellious young man who, after filling the squares required of him by his parents and the Church as a youth, has decided it is "his time" and has openly rebelled against the truths that he once taught on a daily basis.

We work so hard to get our young men and young women to serve full-time missions, and yet when they come home, we pat them on the back, tell them good job, and expect them to find their way to a happy marriage, fatherhood or motherhood, a successful career, and productive Church service with barely any effort. Somehow, we seem to think they no longer need all the attention, encouragement, and teaching of the past. We assume that as returned missionaries they should automatically know what to do.

If we expended such a great deal of effort preparing them for full-time missionary service, why would we think that they will be ready for the difficulties of life without more preparation and guidance?

I have spent much of my career teaching. I spent three years teaching at the Missionary Training Center and five years as an instructor in the Air Force, in the classroom and in the cockpit. For several years, I have trained pilots how to fly the Boeing 737. Learning is a process that never grows old. Learning doesn't care what you have accomplished before. No matter how far you have come in life or what accolades you have earned, learning requires renewed effort.

Late one night, I was instructing two former fighter pilots in the simulator of the B737. Each pilot had over twenty years of experience, had reached the pinnacle of his career, and had achieved honor and rank reserved for only a few. They reeked of confidence and capability. They had earned the respect of their peers, subordinates, and commanders.

You might expect that the first lesson went well, but it didn't. They struggled. They fought with each other. They crashed the simulator several times. They failed to display the basic skills they had learned so many years ago. They looked like a couple of newbies, but then again they were new. They just hadn't realized it yet. They still considered themselves as confident and capable in this new environment as they had been in their old one. They didn't understand that they had much to learn.

When we debriefed, they were as humble as whipped pups. I sat back with my feet up on the table and grinned. These two exceptional pilots had forgotten the sacrifices they had made to get where they were and had become somewhat complacent about their previous achievements and abilities. They had figured if they could fly fighter aircraft, then flying an airliner would be a cakewalk. They were wrong.

I told both of them to go home and to get a good night's rest, and when they awoke the next morning they needed to laugh about their performance the previous night. I assured them that they could fly an airliner but had simply forgotten how to learn. I reminded them that they hadn't reached the pinnacle of their careers without arduous days of learning and practicing. They were quite capable of becoming outstanding airline pilots, but only if they applied the same efforts to their current endeavor as they had in achieving their previous status.

The next night, they were different pilots. They came fully prepared. They learned from their previous mistakes. They helped each other. They pulled from their previous experience. They rediscovered their ability to learn. They had become teachable again.

Newly returned missionaries are like those fighter pilots learning to fly an airliner. They have accomplished amazing things. They were sent into difficult situations and have proven themselves masters of adversity. They have become gospel scholars, excellent teachers, faithful companions, and Christlike leaders. They have earned the respect and adoration of their peers, family, and Church leaders. But they still have a lot to learn.

One recently returned missionary named Wayne Owens expressed it like this: "My mission isn't the most spiritual point of my life. It is a springboard. . . . There is joy in pursuing holiness and discipleship."[1]

Ideally, the mission experience will be a springboard for many other amazing life accomplishments, but not without further effort and continued learning. Returned missionaries who have returned with honor must learn to continue with honor.

THE PURPOSE OF THIS BOOK

THIS BOOK IS an attempt to help you—the wonderful, capable returned missionary—stay in the learning process. It is an effort to help you take advantage of all the hard-learned lessons from your mission. It isn't intended to be abstract information, but rather to be practical advice that can be applied. It is meant to spur action. I hope that this counsel can help keep you on the path of happiness.

The purpose of this book is to help you

- Transition back into everyday life without losing spirituality
- Capture the lessons learned from your missionary experience and apply them to life after the mission
- Set new goals that will carry your life forward
- Rebuild important relationships with family and friends, and develop new ones

- Manage and prioritize the expectations of self, society, and Heavenly Father
- Strive to continue the learning process and remain anxiously engaged

This book is best used when you

- Only read the section that applies to your timeline (in other words, read the section for the first week at the start of your first week home and wait to read the section for the first month until after your first week)
- Take time to accomplish the activities listed
- Involve parents and friends
- Involve your ecclesiastical leaders
- Pray for personal guidance
- Allow yourself room to make mistakes

PARENTS AND LEADERS

Parents: You watch as your son or daughter walks off the airplane and back into the family circle. You feel great pride at his or her service and immense joy at your reunion. It is a day filled with warm embraces, guileless laughter, and sweet tears. You might take a moment to bask in the light that radiates from your son or daughter and swell with pride. Go ahead. Take that victory lap, but only one lap because your work is not done. You have reached an important milestone as a parent, but the race has not been won. You have many miles ahead if you are to endure to the end and claim the prize. In the words of Paul to the Hebrews, "let us run with patience the race that is set before us" (Hebrews 12:1).

So what can you do to best support your returned missionary?

First, understand that your son or daughter will absolutely need your comfort and guidance as he or she transitions back into everyday life. Remember that returned missionaries are grieving. They are grieving the loss of the black name tag. They are grieving the end of full-time service. They are grieving because of the sudden separation from investigators, companions, and all the people they served. It is a strange grief that blindsides them and can send them reeling emotionally. They might feel guilty because at a time when they should be excited about being home, they really wish they could be back in their mission. Like any grieving process, it will take time, but it will go smoother if you are supportive during this process.

Show returned missionaries that they are loved. You may not understand all the emotions they are going through. Their behavior may seem strange, stilted, and perhaps even a bit self-righteous. They may seem moody, distant, and sometimes just downright weird. You would think that after all the support you have given them while they were a full-time missionary that they should know how much you love them, but with all the emotional currents of the moment, they need your love to anchor them. The love you show them will help to ground them emotionally and provide a haven for them to process all their feelings without feeling vulnerable.

Actively listen to them. Don't ask them the simple questions that require only a trite answer. Ask them probing, open-ended questions that require deep thought and evoke deep emotions. Then really listen to their responses. These questions might include

- Who was your favorite companion and why?
- Did you witness any miracles?
- What life lessons did you learn from one of your investigators?
- What was the hardest day of your mission?
- What were the happiest, saddest, and funniest moments of your mission?
- If you could go back and have lunch with one person from your mission, who would it be? Why?

Give returned missionaries room to be the adults they are. Remember, they are not the same people that left home. They have endured hardships, accomplished difficult tasks, and fulfilled roles worthy of adulthood. Don't try to put them back into the mold of the teenager they were in when they left. Let them grow up. Treat them like the adult they are now.

Validate the emotions they are feeling. Professional counselor LuAnn Roundy said, "Even though [returned missionaries are adults] by the world's standards, the part of the brain that processes emotions has just finished developing and they have not obtained the emotional skills that you have. Validating is as easy as listening and then reflecting back to them that what they are thinking, feeling, and experiencing is real, logical, and makes sense. As you validate the emotion, they learn to trust what they feel is real, that others feel it also, and in turn can learn to validate themselves emotionally."[2] Help them feel validated.

Provide them with a home environment conducive to the Spirit. Returned missionaries have spent years avoiding anything that might distract them from the work of salvation for a while. They will feel awkward at home when the TV is on or when music is playing. They will feel lost without daily scripture study.

You are not under any obligation to live according to mission rules, but perhaps you might examine your daily activities against the mission standards and find that you have allowed things into your home that do not invite the Spirit. You might find that your spiritual home needs a bit of spring cleaning. Be the faithful companion they need for scripture study and prayer and ensure a home environment that is conducive to the Spirit.

The homecoming of returned missionaries should be a joyous event that fills you with pride. Bask in the proud parental moment, but be prepared for more parenting. This book is a tool to help your returning missionary continue to apply the successful principles learned during missionary service. Use it to help your son or daughter make a successful transition.

Leaders: Recognize that returned missionaries are going through a transition and, like anyone else, they are vulnerable during this time. The release process is an opportunity for you to assess their spiritual and emotional state. Don't assume that all is well in Zion. Take time during that process to dig a little deeper and discover any needs that might go unfilled during this transition. In speaking of retaining converts, Gordon B. Hinckley once said, "Every one of them needs three things: a friend, a responsibility, and nurturing with 'the good word of God.'"[3] Returned missionaries need the same three things.

Make sure that they have friends they can turn to as they adjust to the next phase of life. In many cases, they will have parents and family as a resource, but not always. They may also have other faithful friends in their home ward or the young single adult ward, but if not, make sure that you assign someone to help guide, mentor, and provide friendship during this critical time in their lives.

Ensure that returned missionaries are put to work quickly. These valiant young men and women have been serving full-time and they will feel a great loss in their lives when they remove the black name tag. Don't think that they need time to recover. Prayerfully consider a calling for them and put them to work right away.

Like the seed of faith described by Alma, returned missionaries need to be nurtured with the good word of God. Ideally, that nurturing will come from family and personal scripture study, but don't assume that it will. Invite them to continue the habits of daily gospel study. Challenge them and their family to search the scriptures together.

Show your love for returned missionaries by actually following up with a visit, or via electronic communication, or by assigning someone to follow up in your stead. Let them know when you interview them that you will be following up and explain the mechanism and timing by which it will be done. This simple act will help them remain true to the covenants they have been teaching. Love them enough to follow up on their progress.

This book is a tool that you can use to guide returned missionaries during this critical time. It is a flexible framework that focuses on three phases: the first week, the first month, and the first year. It includes several activities designed to help them continue in successful gospel pathways. Add this to your leadership toolbox and use it in any way you can to assist those who rely on your counsel.

THE FIRST WEEK: REST, RELATE, REFLECT

O **KAY, YOU HAVE** been released. You no longer have a companion looking over your shoulder. You can hug members of the opposite sex. You don't have any appointments. You can leave your area without getting approval from mission leaders. You can listen to music. You can wear whatever you want. You can go swimming.

What do you do now? For the first week, focus on the four Rs: regulated rest, relate, and reflect.

REGULATED REST

Ask any missionary what he or she wants to do most when home and most likely the answer will be sleep. Missionaries work hard, and if they are keeping the rules they never get enough sleep. It is essential for the returned missionary to recover during the first week through *regulated* rest.

It is important for you to rest from your labors. The first few nights back home can be disruptive to sleep patterns and routine and consequently may keep you from getting proper rest in the right way. You might also still be recovering from jet lag. You have earned the right to a good rest and you should not feel guilty for taking some time to catch up on much needed sleep, but be sure it is regulated.

Manage your bedtime and stick to a sleep schedule in line with gospel principles. Remember the counsel given in Doctrine and Covenants 88:124: "Retire to thy bed early, that ye may not be weary; arise early, that your bodies and your minds may be invigorated." It is easy to slip out of a healthy routine during this transition period. Strive to retire early and keep the same habits you have groomed as a missionary.

If you want to move forward to tackle other difficult tasks in life, you need to give yourself a moment to catch your breath. You need to rest. Take a few days to recover from the long days and short nights of missionary service with regulated rest.

ACTIVITY: Discipline yourself as well as your bedtime. Retire at the same hour you did as a missionary, but then allow yourself to sleep until you wake up naturally. Do this for at least two days of the first week home. Don't feel guilty about it. Let your mind, body, and spirit rest and recover. Then continue the healthy sleep routine as advised in Doctrine and Covenants 88. Doing this will help you start getting back into the swing of things.

RELATE

The Lord counseled Newel K. Whitney to be "more diligent and concerned at home" (D&C 93:50). You have spent numerous hours building relationships of trust, overcoming objections and concerns, and serving people in your mission. Now it is time to apply those same principles to the members of your family, ward, and community.

Take the time to build—or rebuild—relationships with your family members. Use the same principles and techniques that you used with investigators. Serve them. Show genuine concern for their lives. Be sincere in your affection. Spend time with them. Cry at their pain. Laugh with them. Help bear their burdens. You might be surprised to find that your parents have the same struggles with living the gospel as many of your investigators did.

Your friends may need to feel the power of your testimony. Your ward may need your service. Relationships of trust take effort. Put some time and effort into your most important relationships. Expect those relationships to blossom like the relationships you built with your investigators.

ACTIVITY: Spend one-on-one time with each of your parents and siblings. Treat them like a golden investigator. Ask them about their lives, their conversion, and their dreams. Take the time to listen, and be prepared to share the same things with them.

REFLECT

I still hear men with white hair begin a comment in various quorum meetings with the phrase, "While I was on my mission, I learned . . ." Few times in life will the lessons you learn be so poignant as when you were a missionary. If you want to be able to draw from the power of those lessons, you must remember and capture them. You must take time to reflect on them and write them down.

As a missionary, you both wrote home and to your mission president each week. Collect those letters or emails. If you don't have hard copies, print them out and organize them in chronological order. Gather the letters your parents or friends sent to you and put them in a binder. They are precious gems that must be guarded and cherished.

Organize your journal entries. Make sure you have all the pages you wrote in one binder or box. Take some time to review those entries and add other thoughts or explanations to them. Pull valuable experiences out and expand upon them in writing. Share them with your friends, family, or ward members as appropriate. Finish any unfinished stories. Give yourself the time to ponder the events that shaped you and your mission into the valuable experience that it was.

Go through all of your photos. If they are digital, select the best or most memorable ones and get them printed, or bound in a scrapbook. Back them up and preserve them. Put all of your pictures into a movie or slideshow with your own narration. Write down names and information about the people in the photos. Make comments about the events surrounding the photo. A picture is worth a thousand words, but less if it's never shared, or nothing if it's lost. Reflect on your mission as you organize all of your photos.

ACTIVITY: Organize your photos in a format that you can share, and then share them with someone.

ACTIVITY: Write about your transition back to normal life in a journal, making particular note of your emotions about returning home.

ACTIVITY: Use proper social media to reconnect with investigators, companions, and Church members from your mission. Don't live in the past, but use this tool to stay connected to their lives and continue to provide an example with your own.

Reflect on the deep spiritual experiences that carried you through your mission.

- When did you feel the Spirit?
- When did you see the fires of testimony come to life in the eyes of someone you were teaching?
- What miracles did you witness?
- When did your testimony grow significantly?
- Where were you when your bosom burned and your mind was filled with peace and comfort?
- Which interviews with your mission president impacted you the most? Why?

Your mission experience is a reservoir of experiences that can see you through the spiritual droughts that will surely come, but you must make an effort to preserve that precious water if you wish to partake of it later. Take time to reflect on your mission experience and capture those lessons.

ACTIVITY: Prepare three talks or lessons that use an experience from your mission as the focal point.

ACTIVITY: Make a timeline of your mission including key dates and events such as your transfers, baptisms, and mission callings.

ACTIVITY: Do the "Attribute Activity" from *Preach My Gospel* chapter 6 (adjusting the questions to fit your current life situation) and write your answers in your journal so you can reference them later.

During the first week, focus on properly regulated rest, effective relationships, and deep personal reflection.

How did the first week go? Join us on Facebook or Twitter (https://www.facebook.com/ReturnandContinue or @ReturnContinue) and post a picture of your mission, your homecoming, or yourself at the end of your first week (#ReturnandContinue).

NOTES

_____

_____

_____

_____

_____

_____

_____

_____

_____

_____

Return and Continue with Honor

_____

_____

_____

_____

_____

_____

_____

_____

_____

_____

_____

_____

_____

_____

_____

_____

THE FIRST MONTH: GOALS, GAINS, GET BUSY

CONGRATULATIONS, YOU'VE SURVIVED the first week home. You should feel well rested and ready to tackle the next challenge. You should have reconnected with friends and loved ones and actively reflected on your experiences to capture the lessons learned so they are accessible in the future. You are beginning to feel a little more comfortable not putting on the black name tag everyday, but you still feel out of place, like you should be doing something and you just don't know what it is.

The first month home can be difficult, especially if you don't have something worthy of your best effort to focus on. During your first month, you need to set new goals, ensure you maintain the gains that you made as a missionary, and get busy with other worthy endeavors that will challenge and stretch you.

GOALS

"I don't know where I am, but I'm making record time."

—Anonymous WWII pilot
lost over the Pacific Ocean

When navigating across long distances, one degree of directional change equates to a one-mile error every sixty miles of travel. At first that one-degree error doesn't seem like much. Your course is close to where you should be and everything appears to be within tolerances. But as the distance traveled increases, so too does the error in navigation. One degree of change will result in a ten-mile error after six hundred miles—not exactly the straight and narrow path.

The course you set now will determine your future destination, and a minor deviation now, if not corrected, will result in an entirely different destination. Course corrections can be made along the way, but setting the wrong course in the first place can be hazardous.

Setting a goal is like setting the proper course in a plane. Heavenly Father has stated His goal and purpose: "For behold, this is my work and my glory—to bring to pass the immortality and eternal life of man" (Moses 1:39). His course is "one eternal round" and His "paths are straight" (D&C 3:2). Heavenly Father has a plan. If the Creator of the universe sets goals and outlines His direction, perhaps you should do the same.

The unifying theme of serving a full-time mission has dominated your life for almost as long as you can remember. What do you focus on now that you have achieved that goal? Is there anything else worthy of so much preparation and dedication? Yes!

President David O. McKay said, "No other success can compensate for failure in the home."[4] Believe it or not, this applies to your success as a missionary as well. Any success you achieved as a missionary is secondary to the journey you are about to embark on. Like the two seasoned pilots mentioned earlier, you have achieved great things, but the greater prize lies ahead. Just like the goal of serving a full-time mission guided and shaped your youth, temple marriage and an eternal family are the themes that should shape the rest of your life.

As a missionary, you learned to set goals. Every week, you sat down and discussed your companionship goals. Every week, you reported your progress to your mission leaders. You regularly met with your mission president and discussed your progress in personal and mission goals. You set goals as a mission, a zone, and a district. You had personal study goals. You had teaching goals. You had goals for your investigators.

Goal setting was an integral part of your life as a missionary. If goal setting was important for a successful missionary experience, wouldn't you agree that it will be essential for a successful life *after* your mission?

During the first month back, take time to ponder your future and set some long-term goals. Contemplate where you would like to be ten, twenty, and even fifty years down the road. With the overarching theme of the eternal family as your guiding principle, consider things like vocation, education, financial needs and wants, establishing a home, starting a family, and a career. You will serve in multiple roles in life. To fulfill each of these roles, you will need clear goals in each area.

Spend some time pondering your future. Outline the things you want to accomplish with your life. Dream big. Make plans for the next fifty or more years. Consider the things you wish to accomplish before you pass away. Take heed to the counsel given by prophets concerning success in life. What do you want people to say about you at your funeral? Determine your course and set goals worthy of your best efforts.

A good goal should be

- Believable (something that you believe you can accomplish)
- Achievable (something that can actually be done)
- Measurable (you must be able to measure your progress)
- Written (a goal not written is just a wish)
- Dated (a goal must have timelines)
- Flexible (make room for setbacks, adjustments, and changes)

For more information about goals, refer to "Setting Goals and Managing Time" in the manual *The Gospel and the Productive Life*.[5]

ACTIVITY: Write the eulogy you would like someone to give at your funeral that outlines all of your greatest accomplishments in life. Who will you be? What will you have done? Whose lives will you have touched? How did you spend your time?

ACTIVITY: Set a long-term goal (such as graduate from college, own your own business, buy a home) and break the goal down into long, intermediate, short-term, and daily goals and tasks. Determine what you can do this month, this week, and today to accomplish that goal, and then do it!

ACTIVITY: Talk to someone who has accomplished one of the goals you want to accomplish and share your plan with them. Listen and apply their advice if it is good.

GAINS

Captain Moroni knew the importance of keeping captured territory. "Yea, and it became expedient that we should employ our men to the maintaining those parts of the land which we had regained of our possessions" (Alma 58:3). He understood that it was easier to maintain conquered territory than to lose it because of carelessness and have to regain it. He understood the value of a secured position.

✱ **ACTIVITY:** Make a list of all the spiritual, emotional, and intellectual gains that you have made during you time as a missionary. Outline the areas where you have grown the most.

If Captain Moroni, one of the great strategists of the scriptures, felt it expedient to maintain conquered ground, how should you feel about the gains you have made? Are you happier because of your growth? Are you more capable because of your improvements? Would you like to maintain those lessons learned or have to learn them all over again? It is expedient that you maintain the ground you've gained over the course of missionary service.

Being a missionary takes a lot of self-discipline. You have learned the value of discipline, habits, and routine. You have learned to be accountable to someone else. Every worthwhile endeavor, no matter how pleasing it might be, will require a certain measure of discipline to accomplish. You have learned that. Why would it be any different as you move forward? A life well lived will require discipline, primarily self-discipline. Thomas S. Monson said, "Eternal life in the kingdom of our Father is your goal, and self-discipline will surely be required if you are to achieve it."[6]

Carlos E. Asay taught this to his missionaries who were about to return home:

As missionaries completed their work in the Texas North Mission, where I served, I would invite them to sit down, to reflect, and to list all of the habits which they felt they had acquired during their terms of service. Most lists would include phrases like this:

- The habit of rising and retiring early.
- The habit of praying frequently.
- The habit of studying the scriptures regularly.
- The habit of exercising daily.
- The habit of working hard, consistently—and on and on it would go.

When the list was complete, I would ask the missionary to identify those habits which he felt he should break and discard upon his return home and his subsequent release. Nearly every missionary would eye his list carefully and respond something like this: "President, I can see only one habit which I can afford to place aside."

"What is that?" I would ask.

Invariably the missionary would conclude, "I can drop my daily tracting."[7]

How do you maintain the personal ground you have gained during your time as a missionary? You must apply the same principles that helped you progress as a missionary: self-discipline, accountability, routine, and righteous habits.

Organize your time so that you don't slip back into the habits of youth, where you were perhaps wandering in the wilderness without direction. Establish a weekly schedule to help you stay focused. Your schedule should include

- Appropriate times to go to bed and get up in the morning
- Personal scripture study, daily prayers, and temple attendance
- Fulfilling and magnifying any calling you might receive
- Self-improvement
- Learning or school
- Fun and recreation
- Social activities

ACTIVITY: Write out your daily and weekly schedule. Include enough time for scripture study, personal prayers, self-improvement, and fun. Put your schedule in a visible place and do your best to stick to it.

Be accountable to someone. Accountability gives energy to goals, heightens the sense of urgency and importance, and gives weight to personal commitments. If you wish to continue your growth, find someone to be accountable to. President Thomas S. Monson said, "When performance is measured, performance improves. When performance is measured and reported, the rate of improvement accelerates."[8] Accountability will accelerate your successes.

Ralph Waldo Emerson once said, "Our chief want is someone who will inspire us to be what we know we could be."[9] Within the structure of the Church you have several resources for accountability: your bishop, quorum leaders, Relief Society leaders, home teachers, visiting teachers, or other Church members. You also have the members of your family to draw from: parents, siblings, cousins, aunts, uncles, or perhaps grandparents. Or maybe you feel more comfortable being accountable to a friend.

Whomever you choose, make sure they have your best interests at heart, they share a similar vision for success in life, and they lift you up and expect the best of you.

ACTIVITY: Find someone you trust to share your goals with. Ask them to hold you accountable and report back to them regularly.

It is important and beneficial for you to maintain the ground that you have gained from your time as a missionary, but don't loiter on the "okay plateau." Recognize the possibility that previous problems may need continued effort to face and overcome. Don't expect perfection in an imperfect world, but don't settle for okay either. Strive for excellence. Decide to be better today than you were yesterday. Even if you are on the right path, you will still get run over if you aren't moving. Strive to move forward each day with self-discipline, a consistent and healthy routine, and regular accountability. Don't lose the precious ground you have gained.

GET BUSY

There is danger in a lack of purpose. There is trouble in a lack of direction. Idle hands are indeed the devil's workshop. Consider the story of King David's downfall. Instead of leading his men into battle, he remained back in his palace "at the time when kings go forth to battle" (2 Samuel 11:1). Then he was restless one night and wandered around on his rooftop, looking down on the surrounding houses. He saw a woman bathing. From that encounter, he committed adultery and colluded to have her husband, Uriah, killed in battle so that he could take Bath-sheba as his wife. It all started with a lack of purpose, and perhaps not attending to duties. There is danger in idleness.

As a missionary, your days were programmed and filled with assignments. Now you may find yourself wandering around on the rooftop with idle time on your hands. You may have slipped back into or been victim to the idleness traps that were waiting to ensnare you: entertainment, gaming, sports, hobbies, or even pornography. Most of these activities are good and wholesome (except pornography) when balanced with industry and purpose, but when you indulge yourself and fill all of your idle time with pleasure and fun, a sense of emptiness and low self-esteem begins to creep into life and debilitates you.

How do you avoid the idleness traps? Become "anxiously engaged in a good cause" (D&C 58:27). Wholesome recreation (in proper proportion), service, work, self-improvement, and education are activities that will help you put your idle time to good use. If you don't proactively fill your time with good causes, it will surely get filled with things that matter little or have little eternal value.

So fill your free time with good causes, with things that are praiseworthy or of good report. You have much to accomplish in your life. You have much to do and in less time than you might think. Don't let your time go to waste. The following is a list of possible activities to keep you anxiously engaged.

- Working on a creative project
- Temple visits
- Wholesome hobbies in proper measure
- Spending time with family and friends
- Church calling and home or visiting teaching
- Developing talents
- Learning from and reading good books
- Working on your résumé
- Filling out job applications

- Going to interviews (even if it's just practice)
- Visiting or researching potential schools
- Looking into potential careers
- Trying out and learning new skills
- Family history work
- Serving in the community

This isn't meant as an all-inclusive list. As disciples of Christ, we don't have time for idleness. "The harvest truly is great, but the labourers are few" (Luke 10:2). Avoid the idleness traps by thrusting your sickle with all of your might into worthy things. Replace any idle time you may have with productive, praiseworthy activities that will both enlighten the mind and enrich the soul. Get busy!

ACTIVITY: Spend at least three hours in the service of others this week. Visit justserve.org and look for service opportunities.

ACTIVITY: Make a list of productive things to do with your time. When you find yourself idle, pull out the list and accomplish one or two of the items. (If you need help with the list, get suggestions from your bishop, father, mother, or other leaders.)

The first month after your mission is a critical time. It is the perfect time to set new goals, ensure that you hold onto the gains you have made, and get busy with worthwhile endeavors.

How did the first month go? Join us on Facebook or Twitter (https://www.facebook.com/ReturnandContinue or @ReturnContinue) and tell us about one of your new goals. Take a picture that represents a new aspiration or direction (#ReturnandContinue).

NOTES

_____

_____

_____

_____

_____

_____

_____

_____

_____

_____

Return and Continue with Honor

_____

_____

_____

_____

_____

_____

_____

_____

_____

_____

_____

_____

_____

_____

THE FIRST YEAR: ADJUST SOCIALLY, ADVANCE INTELLECTUALLY, APPLY SPIRITUALLY

CONGRATULATIONS, YOU'VE MADE it through the first month. With any luck, you are grounded in the lessons you learned as a missionary and have focused on the horizon of great things to come. You should start to feel a new sense of purpose and sense of direction.

Maybe you have a new job, calling, or semester to keep you busy. Maybe you've begun to feel comfortable in your new setting and in your new roles, but you still find yourself overcome with an awkward feeling from time to time. That awkward feeling is normal. It is often the by-product of having served a faithful mission. The first year will be a time of adjustment, advancement, and application.

Think back on the *first* lesson that you taught as a missionary. Did you feel nervous? Insecure? Did you struggle with the new language or simply with putting coherent sentences together? If you were at all like most missionaries, it was definitely an awkward time. Now think back on your *last* lesson. Did you feel confident in your abilities? Did you feel strong in your testimony? Were you afraid of handling objections? If you were like most missionaries, by the end of your mission teaching the gospel was second nature.

What was the difference between the first lesson and the last? Was the task easier? Did the investigator pose fewer difficult questions, doubts, or objections? Had gospel principles changed and suddenly become easier to teach?

Ralph Waldo Emerson said, "That which we persist in doing becomes easier for us to do—not that the nature of the thing has changed, but that our power to do has increased."[10] As a missionary, you grew over time to fill the role and meet the responsibilities placed upon you. It took an incredible amount of effort, perseverance, and reliance on the Lord to develop your skills and talents. All that doesn't end after the mission.

You have several tasks ahead of you that may seem daunting: dating and marriage, getting an education, developing a marketable skill or vocation, starting a career, and establishing a home of your own. These are difficult tasks, but with practice you can increase your capacity and power to accomplish them. Even Jesus

Christ Himself "increased in wisdom and stature, and in favour with God and man" (Luke 2:52).

Christ grew line upon line in three areas: socially ("favour with man"), intellectually ("wisdom and stature"), and spiritually ("favour with God"). Likewise, you will need to grow in the same three areas. During your first year, you should adjust socially, advance intellectually, and apply spiritually.

ADJUST SOCIALLY

A friend of mine returned from faithful missionary service only to find that his casual clothing didn't fit anymore and was slightly out of style. He went to the local mall to purchase items for his wardrobe before returning to school. The sales clerk helping him was a cute young woman, and he immediately felt awkward.

He selected a few items to try on, and when he exited the dressing room to look in the mirror, the helpful sales clerk stood nearby. When he asked about the sizing of the waistband of the jeans, the sales clerk grabbed the waistband and tugged to check the fit. Though the contact was not intended as a romantic gesture, my friend later joked that he was instantly in love and ready for marriage.

Perhaps you have felt similar feelings concerning contact with members of the opposite sex after avoiding physical contact as a missionary. Perhaps you have felt awkward and clumsy in social settings, or you have also felt a surge in emotion uncharacteristic for the social interaction that is actually taking place. These are all normal feelings, considering that as a missionary you avoided close contact with the opposite sex and social events that were not gospel-centered. So just as Jesus himself grew in favor with others, you will need to grow and adjust socially to feel comfortable in several social settings.

Social skills, like any skill, can be learned, and if they are to be mastered they must also be practiced. They require a measure of learning and effort to improve. As a missionary, you increased and improved your social skills by interacting with members, investigators, and total strangers. You learned to develop relationships of trust by displaying sincere interest and concern for those you were teaching. You learned to overcome objections through inspired questions. You learned to break down walls of doubt with charitable service. You developed all of these abilities through conscious effort and continued practice.

One difference exists between the social skills you developed as a missionary and the social skills you need as a returned missionary: intent.

As a missionary, you developed and used your social skills to find people to teach. As a returned missionary, you will use your social skills to find lifelong friends. As a missionary, you developed relationships to further the work of the Lord. As a returned missionary, you develop relationships to help you find gainful employment. As a missionary, you invested time and effort into others so they would feel your sincerity and listen to your message. As a returned missionary, you invest in others so you have loyal friends who stand by you during your own times of need. As a missionary, you developed relationships of trust so that others could develop their own faith. As a returned missionary, you develop relationships of trust so that a member of the opposite sex will have enough faith in you to marry you.

The skills you need as a returned missionary are similar to the skills you developed as a missionary, but they must be employed in different settings and with different intent.

Think back again to the first few weeks and months of your missionary service. Did it feel normal striking up a conversation with a total stranger (perhaps even in a foreign language)? Did it feel comfortable expressing your love for someone you had only recently met? Did it feel natural offering to serve someone you barely knew? And yet by the end of your missionary service you were comfortable with all of those applied skills and principles. It was simply a matter of practice.

You will not develop or learn to apply your social skills in new social settings unless you put yourself in those settings. In other words, you will need to get out of your comfort zone a bit. How do you do that? Attend Church activities. Participate in wholesome recreation with others. Have meaningful conversations with others. Reenter the dating scene by inviting someone (or by accepting someone's invitation) to go on a date. You have the basic skills necessary to adjust socially, but like a muscle that doesn't get used often, those skills will atrophy over time if they are not used.

You will most likely feel awkward with members of the opposite sex. Consider all your interactions with members of the opposite sex during your mission and you will understand why. As a missionary, you were not allowed to date, have close contact with, or interact in any manner that might promote romantic feelings of love. You strongly guarded your heart and checked your emotions to properly serve. Unlocking those emotions and allowing them space will feel awkward at first, but if you are to move forward with the most important work of life—marriage and family—you will need to date, form a close bond, and eventually develop feelings of love.

However, do be cautious and avoid applying your commitment skills to every dating relationship. As a missionary, every person you met needed to hear your message. Because of the universality of your message, you naturally tried to increase the level of commitment of everyone you spoke with. The habit of increasing commitment in everyone you meet can hinder dating relationships. You'll need your social skills in dating, but you must resist the urge to commit everyone you date to the next level. It will take effort to start relationships, but good relationships will grow naturally without a lot of effort, other than the time you invest.

It's easy to step outside the bounds the Lord has set for chastity during this awkward time. You are unleashing strong emotions that have been restrained and they will often come rushing out in waves so strong they threaten to overpower you. Move slowly and set boundaries. Interact in groups before dating one-on-one. When you date, choose an activity that you are comfortable with and that allows you interact emotionally instead of simply being close to one another physically. Recognize that passion is a natural progression of a growing relationship that has to be checked by the Lord's standards. If you hope to have a healthy and loving marital relationship, you will have to maintain respect for chastity as you date.

Cultivate friendships through wholesome recreation, hobbies, and entertainment. Develop your social skills by attending various Church activities. Adjust socially by interacting with the opposite sex in appropriate ways and settings. Just as Christ Himself did, you also will increase your social skills through practice and patience.

ACTIVITY: Attend a Church activity and meet five new people. Exchange contact information and follow up with those you felt drawn to the most.

ACTIVITY: Go on a group date. Plan or suggest an activity that can allow for interaction on several levels. Avoid putting too much pressure on the activity and allow the interaction between everyone involved to develop naturally.

ACTIVITY: Find a recreational activity or hobby that you enjoy. Invite others to join.

ACTIVITY: Reach out to someone in a social setting who appears to be isolated from the group. Find out more about him or her and make an effort to help him or her feel included.

ADVANCE INTELLECTUALLY

It is impossible to serve a faithful mission without getting smarter. No doubt you learned to speak better, read better, and write better. You learned about the world around you, about people, places, and things you didn't even know existed before. You expanded your thinking and your vision of the world you live in. Like Christ, who grew in wisdom with age, you learned to reason both spiritually and intellectually. Perhaps more important, you developed good study habits and learning skills. You are smarter today than the day you left, but you will not continue to get smarter unless you continue to focus on learning and challenging yourself intellectually.

As members of the Church, we believe that "the glory of God is intelligence, or, in other words, light and truth" (D&C 93:36). We also believe that "whatever principle of intelligence we attain unto in this life, it will rise with us in the resurrection. And if a person gains more knowledge and intelligence in this life through his diligence and obedience than another, he will have so much the advantage in the world to come" (D&C 130:18–19). When we gain knowledge and intelligence, it not only helps us in the world to come, but also in this world. We value education. As said in the pamphlet *For the Strength of Youth*,

> Education is an investment that brings great rewards and will open the doors of opportunity that may otherwise be closed to you. Plan now to obtain an education. Be willing to work diligently and make sacrifices if necessary. Share your educational goals with your family, friends, and leaders so they can support and encourage you. Maintain an enthusiasm for learning throughout your life. Find joy in continuing to learn and in expanding your interests. Choose to actively participate in the learning opportunities available to you.[11]

Learning is a process that should never end. Like the previously mentioned seasoned fighter pilots learning to fly the airliner, you have proven your ability to learn, but that doesn't mean you have learned everything you need to know about life. Not by a long shot. Challenge yourself by seeking out more advanced education. And recognize that your life's education is only just beginning. Advance intellectually by seeking "out of the best books words of wisdom; seek learning, even by study and also by faith" (D&C 88:118).

As Latter-day Saints, one advantage we have is the power of the Holy Ghost to help us learn. Jesus taught His disciples that the Comforter would "bring all things to your remembrance" (John 14:26). What a powerful tool for helping us increase our intelligence. Of course, that gift works best when we are striving to be worthy of it through our obedience. Likewise, the Holy Ghost cannot fill an empty mind. Elder Royden G. Derrick explained,

> Sometimes, in response to our prayers, the Holy Spirit puts new thoughts in our minds. In my experience, this happens very seldom. Most of the time, he takes thoughts from the storehouse of one's own brain and brings them forward for review. Thus, it is important that we study and fill our minds with knowledge and learning about things as they were, as they are, and as they are to come. The Spirit cannot bring thoughts to recall from an empty mind.[12]

You'll need to study in order to advance intellectually. Ideally, you should seek out formal schooling to develop marketable skills that you can use to support and bless your future family, but if your resources are limited, make the most of what you have. Learning comes in various forms, but it always requires "diligence and obedience" (D&C 130:19).

Explore low-cost options like community colleges, distance learning, or vocational or technical schools. Seek out financial aid through scholarships, grants, or work programs. If you lack resources to attend formal schooling right now, find the library and check out books in your area of interest. Visit free Internet sites such Kahn Academy, Ted Talks, or university sites that offer free learning to willing students with an Internet connection. You may not have the resources for school, but that should not stop you from advancing your intellect.

As a returned missionary, you can use your learning skills to embark on a journey of learning that will keep your life interesting until the day you die, or until you stop learning. The choice is up to you. Make this first year a time to advance intellectually and continue in that course throughout your entire life.

ACTIVITY: Come up with a plan for obtaining more education or vocational training. Seek out advice from leaders, family members, and people you trust to help you advance your education and vocational skills.

ACTIVITY: If you learned a foreign language during your mission, continue to study it and improve your proficiency. Take an advanced course in the language.

ACTIVITY: Choose a school subject that you struggled with before you served. Prayerfully consider how you can improve in that subject. Apply the study skills you learned as a missionary to learning the chosen subject.

ACTIVITY: As advised in the scriptures, seek out the best books. Read a good book each month and discuss it with a friend or family member.

APPLY SPIRITUALLY

Serving as a missionary has laid a sound spiritual foundation. Your innumerable hours spent in personal, companion, and group study have built that foundation brick upon brick, but the house is not finished.

As mentioned earlier, your experience as a missionary should be a springboard for continued spiritual growth throughout your life, but it can't be unless you apply the same efforts, habits, and principles that led to spiritual growth as a missionary. In your efforts to grow spiritually, you will find that what you lack is not knowledge or understanding. You merely lack application. Your environment has changed, but you will have many opportunities to apply gospel principles to everyday life. If you are to continue to grow spiritually as a returned missionary, you must apply spiritually.

Think back for a moment about a time during your mission when you experienced spiritual growth. Where were you? Who was your companion? What were your daily habits? How did you know you were growing spiritually? Was that particular experience ever repeated during your mission? Maybe go back and read a journal entry about the experience.

As a missionary, your spiritual growth was almost so commonplace that you may not have even recognized it after a while, but if you take time to ponder, you will see that growth. You will see that, like Paul, you "spake as a child, [you] understood as a child, [you] thought as a child," but now you have "put away childish things" (1 Corinthians 13:11). You will see that you grew by spiritual leaps and bounds.

Where are you spiritually? What are your spiritual strengths and gifts? What are your spiritual weaknesses? How is that spirituality measured? In this process, do not confuse Church activity with spirituality. It's possible to be active in the Church and yet find yourself inactive spiritually. Spirituality is different from mere activity. It requires an internal devotion without any real external motivation. It requires you to accept the Spirit as your guide (see D&C 45:57) and that you "put your trust in that Spirit which leadeth to do good—yea, to do justly, to walk humbly, to judge righteously" (D&C 11:12).

ACTIVITY: Write up a list of your spiritual strengths and gifts. Ponder how you developed them. Make a plan for increasing those strengths through spiritual devotion.

ACTIVITY: Read from your missionary journal. Focus on a time when you grew spiritually. What helped you grow? How did that growth change you as a person? How can you repeat that process?

As a missionary, you became a gospel scholar and taught others multiple gospel principles, but much of that personal knowledge has not been truly tested in the crucible of life. Inevitably though, it will be tested and tried.

Consider the story of Job. At the beginning of his story, he was faithful, righteous, and revered, but he had not been tested to the fulness of his capabilities. He lost his children, his wealth, and his health. Those who should have comforted him reviled him, and his own wife told him to "curse God, and die" (Job 2:9). Job's faith was strengthened in the crucible of affliction, and in the end he testified, "Oh that my words were now written! oh that they were printed in a book! That they were graven with an iron pen and lead in the rock for ever! For I know that my redeemer liveth, and that he shall stand at the latter day upon the earth: And though after my skin worms destroy this body, yet in my flesh shall I see God" (Job 19:23–26).

Like Job, you have acquired tremendous gospel knowledge and accomplished great things. I am not suggesting that difficulties are always necessary for you to grow, but perhaps greater things await you that will only be revealed through unexpected trials of faith. If you are to grow and thrive during those trials, you must learn to *apply* the gospel knowledge you both learned and taught.

The gospel of Jesus Christ—if nothing else—is a rather practical gospel. Repentance allows us to improve. Forgiveness brings us peace in a troubled world. The law of tithing brings financial blessings. The Lord's laws of health improve our health and well-being. Sabbath day observance provides us with a reservoir of strength in stressful times. Each principle is designed to make us wealthier, healthier, and happier, but they will not work if we do not apply them.

It is not uncommon to face doubts during this time of transition. Any rational person will face some doubts. But when you do experience those moments of spiritual confusion or doubt, actively seek answers from reliable spiritual sources. Search and study the scriptures and the teachings of modern prophets. Talk with a mentor, such as a parent or Church leader, who has a vested interest in your spiritual success. Be patient as you search for answers and do not abandon those truths you acquired through your previous learning.

Spiritual growth is impossible without the infinite Atonement of Jesus Christ. Faith in Jesus Christ is the first principle of the gospel by design because none of the other principles have the power to stand alone. Anytime we wish to grow spiritually, we must begin with faith in the Atonement. Howard W. Hunter once said, "None of us has attained perfection or the zenith of spiritual growth that is possible in mortality. Every person can and must make spiritual progress. The gospel of Jesus Christ is the divine plan for that spiritual growth eternally."[13]

Now is the time to apply the spiritual lessons you learned during your mission. Life will provide you with opportunities to apply gospel principles and test your commitment to the truth. Apply the spiritual lessons you learned on your mission, strive to always be worthy of the Spirit, and follow to promptings you receive. Continue to grow spiritually by centering your life on Jesus Christ and the Atonement.

ACTIVITY: Go to the temple while fasting and go with a spiritual question in mind. Ponder it and listen for the whisperings of the Holy Ghost. Act on any promptings that you receive and write down any spiritual lessons in your journal.

What did you accomplish during the first year home from your mission? Join us on Facebook or on Twitter (https://www.facebook.com/ReturnandContinue or @ReturnContinue) and tell us about one of your accomplishments. Take a picture that represents your achievement (#ReturnandContinue).

NOTES

_____

_____

_____

_____

_____

_____

_____

_____

_____

_____

_____

_____

_____

Return and Continue with Honor

_____

_____

_____

_____

_____

_____

_____

_____

_____

_____

_____

_____

_____

MADE IT THROUGH THE FIRST YEAR—NOW WHAT?

YOU HAVE BEEN home for one year. Reflect on the changes and struggles the past year has brought. If you feel further away from Heavenly Father, who moved? If His voice is more difficult to hear, why? What has caused you to feel further from Him? What distractions, shortcomings, or transgressions are keeping you from His blessings? Or, if it is the opposite, what habits or new goals drew you closer to Him and His blessings?

One of the ongoing challenges that you will face is drift. "For the natural man is an enemy to God, and has been from the fall of Adam, and will be, forever and ever, unless he yields to the enticings of the Holy Spirit" (Mosiah 3:19). It is natural for us to drift away from our Heavenly Father because of distractions, shortcomings, sin, or even open rebellion. We must constantly strive to keep ourselves on the straight and narrow path.

A year ago, you walked off the plane with a content look in your eye and an anxious look on your face. You were confident and yet unsettled. You had finished your mission and arrived home to a place that was not as familiar as before.

What did you come home to? More important, what did you make of the home you returned to? Did you come home and continue to serve those around you, or did you fall back into your previous role as a child and only allow yourself to be served? Did you continue to behave like the mature adult you developed into as a missionary, or did you slip back into the old habits of teenage life? Did you return with honor only to watch that honor fade over time due to lack of effort and focus, or did you continue to practice that honor?

If you want to maintain the luster that followed you off the airplane a year ago, you must remain anxiously engaged. You returned with honor, now *continue with honor*.

Consider the words of Nephi as written in 2 Nephi 31:19–20:

> And now, my beloved brethren, after ye have gotten into this strait and narrow path, I would ask if all is done? Behold, I say unto you, Nay; for ye have

not come thus far save it were by the word of Christ with unshaken faith in him, relying wholly upon the merits of him who is mighty to save.

Wherefore, ye must press forward with a steadfastness in Christ, having a perfect brightness of hope, and a love of God and of all men. Wherefore, if ye shall press forward, feasting upon the word of Christ, and endure to the end, behold, thus saith the Father: Ye shall have eternal life.

You are invited to capture the lessons you learned during your missionary service, set new goals, advance intellectually and socially, and apply yourself spiritually. Your mission may have been the most wonderful part of your life so far, but many greater things await you if you will continue with honor.

ACTIVITY: Look over the answers from the "Attribute Activity" from *Preach My Gospel* chapter 6 that you did when you first came home and measure your progress. If necessary, adjust and set new goals.

ACTIVITY: Say a prayer of thanks to Heavenly Father for the things you learned on your mission and ask for His continued daily guidance and help in using those lessons you learned as a springboard for the rest of your life.

ACTIVITY: Press forward feasting upon the word of Christ and strive to always continue your life with honor.

Will you continue with honor? Join us on Facebook or on Twitter (https://www.facebook.com/Returnand-Continue or @ReturnContinue) and let us know that you continued with honor your first year home. Take a picture that represents your commitment to continue with honor (#ContinueWithHonor).

ENDNOTES

1. Marianne H. Prescott, "Returned Missionaries Need a Friend, a Responsibility, and Spiritual Nourishment," *Church News*. February 18, 2014.
2. LuAnn Roundy, interview by Brock Booher, August 19, 2014.
3. Gordon B. Hinckley, "Converts and Young Men," *Ensign*, May 1997.
4. David O. McKay, "The Noble Calling of Parents," from *Teachings of Presidents of the Church* (Salt Lake City: Intellectual Reserve, 2003).
5. "Setting Goals and Managing Time," from *The Gospel and the Productive Life: Student Manual: Religion 150* (Salt Lake City: The Church of Jesus Christ of Latter-day Saints, 2004).
6. Thomas S. Monson, "Pathways to Perfection," *Ensign*, May 2002.

7. Carlos E. Asay, "Flaxen Threads" (presentation, BYU Devotional, Provo, Utah, February 1982).

8. Thomas S. Monson, in Conference Report, October 1970, 107.

9. "Ralph Waldo Emerson Quote." BrainyQuote. Accessed on November 16, 2014, http://www.brainyquote.com/quotes/quotes/r/ralph-waldo130588.html.

10. Quoted by Leon R. Hartshorn, "Heber J. Grant: A Man without Excuses," *New Era*, January 1972.

11. *For the Strength of Youth: Fulfilling Our Duty to God* (Salt Lake City: Intellectual Reserve, 2001), 9–10.

12. Royden G. Derrick. "Agency" (presentation, BYU Devotional, Provo, Utah, June 1983).

13. Howard W. Hunter. "Developing Spirituality," *Ensign*, May 1979.

ABOUT THE AUTHOR

BROCK BOOHER GREW up on a farm in rural Kentucky, the fourth of ten children, where he learned to work hard, use his imagination, and always believe in himself. He served a full-time mission in Uruguay, graduated from BYU, and convinced his wife, Britt, to marry him. They have six children, two of whom have served missions thus far. He began his flying career in the US Air Force and now flies for a major US airline. He has served in various Church capacities and loves teaching. He also writes fiction and has published two novels: *Healing Stone* and *The Charity Chip*. You can find him on Facebook (AuthorBrockBooher) and on Twitter (@BrockBooher) or visit his website, *BrockBooher.com*.